BRINGING EVERYTHING HOME

Previously published poetry

Imaginings (1961)
Putnam

Against the Cruel Frost (1962)
Putnam

Object Relations (1967)
Methuen

Old World New World (1978)
Rapp and Whiting

Chance of a Lifetime (1978)
Anvil

Selected Poems (1980)
Anvil

BRINGING EVERYTHING HOME

David Holbrook

halfacrown

h a l f a c r o w n

First published in Great Britain in 1999
by halfacrown publishers
198 Victoria Avenue
Kingston upon Hull HU5 3DY

Printed in Great Britain by
Copytech UK, Peterborough

ISBN 0 9537022 27

This copy is one of the first 100 copies of the print run.

Acknowledgements

Acknowledgements are due to the editors of the following magazines in which some of these poems first appeared:

Rialto,
The London Magazine,
Outposts,
English,
The Critical Quarterly,
Stand,
The Times Literary Supplement,
Psychopoetica,
New Poetry Nos 6 and 9 (the Arts Council)

Poems have also appeared in a Festschrift for James Hogg and Jack Lindsay.

CONTENTS

Sunday Night, Cambridge Station

In the blackness, the red-eyed signals glow,
A hulk lumbers with doleful twin lamps:
November night at the railway station.
As the Cambridge couples kiss and part
I hug my daughter and her bundled boys.

Clouds of white steam catching the sullen lights
Blow in my momentary dream as my heart plunges
Back to my Blackdown days and the 'forty-eight',
My buff pass buttoned in my chest pocket:
The crowds that were here then, suffering,
Clinging and mooning, with the clatter of boots,
The men bundled with gritty helmets and packs.

And a woman's face close to mine, aware
That this was the end of the affair
With the sleepy cadet in coarse serge, stiff
With the ropes and the drills and the cordite smoke
While she, still in the land of the free and frill,
Was slipping like Cressida into more secure arms.

I hear the whistle blow, and the vapour hiss
And take my last warm desperate kiss
As we choke farewells, blinded by tears and steam.

Well, it was all better in the end, when the wounds
Healed, hells later: but at bewildered nineteen
As our warm rucked bed receded down the line
To the unkind green light the very last time
My spirit died out of me, Underground and Aldershot,
And bit into the earth on the toxin of separation.

I am not checking in at 11.59 hours
At the dismal guardroom in the forest clearing:
This is my garden: I cross it like a fugitive
From another life; for a moment I hardly know you
And have to wind back so many landscapes,
Black nights and charred passages,
Before I can feel safe and glad, and at last shudder
Off the faint nightmare and the distant signal.

Blackdown: a pre-OCTU training camp
'Forty-eight': forty-eight hours leave, from 11.59 hours on Friday until
11.59 hours on Sunday night.

Exit

The coffin is brought in, and I see you are trembling
Beside me, down there, in the crush of people,
Your hands plucking at one another
As they do when you are agitated.
Man's beauty, they sing, fades like moths fretting a garment:
Well, he is gone, your colleague, suddenly:
The press gathers to share its grief – so many!

I fix my eyes on the stained glass figures
Soaring above our heads in the college chapel:
I note that some images are better than others,
The beards more finely delineated, the faces
Human and real, while others are sickly dolls:
I wonder what I mean?

                        Did he believe it,
Really, that we shall meet in another place?
Bitter truth touches us, of being-unto-death:
From the tormented faces etched in the best glass,
From harmonies that utter the figures of our condition:
How one can be here, laughing and gesticulating
Outside the college gates, then, the next week,
Carried out of them in a case to the sound of the choir
Half heard between the gusts of wind and the noise of traffic?

Monteverdi's Vespers

Nivem sicut lanam: there's snow in your hair.
Liquifaciet: it glistens on your cheeks like tears.
You are the more beautiful to me, because
I have been weeping at Monteverdi's choruses
About Mary, *Stella Maris*: the echoes
Seem to come from the fantastic far-away St Mark's
And in the Cambridge scene, I see Venice in snow.

I wish I could believe in Mary, *Virgo Pura*;
I should like to be converted to Christianity:
Monteverdi nearly does it, with his trillos,
But it is too late. Can all these people,
The lean tenors and the flute-toned sopranos,
Can they all believe in a next world
From where the Angel Gabriel spoke to a woman,
The pure reversal of Eve, a gateway to heaven,
By the absolution and atonement of our sins?

In the dark storm, I defer in dread
To the mystery of existence, in my trauma,
Shaking to the acknowledgement of my mortality.

But there is no comfort for me, not even
In the face that I love under the onslaught of ice,
Distant influence that you are, which I orbit.

Yet, there, in yourself, shivering at the voice-shakes,
Only human and as unable to believe as I am –
So that the wool-like snow and our tears melt down
together.

Man Friday

'This thing of darkness I acknowledge mine…'– Prospero.

He collects all the traumas:
He has a hut where he lurks, stinking.
Between two torn-off boughs, he hangs
A plaited rope of hair, and decorates it
With fetishes and offerings, old teeth,
Old bits of fingernails and bandages.

As the Old Year closes in, the darkness
Falls in the early afternoon, his eyes
Go stark with horror, he crouches
With his hands over his eyes, blinking,
Waiting in expectancy for the awful
Unwinding of the earth's orbit into a black
Hole for ever, and everything inside him
Goes wrong, his bladder, his kidneys:
He wakes in sweat all night in dread,
Dying a thousand deaths, moaning.

I have no control over him: I wait
Patiently trying to contain the damage.
At the end of the first week in January
I see a Turkish snowdrop, fully out
In the Botanic Gardens, in the sunlight.
(He leaves his hut for the first time,
Dances outside it, the fool, in bare feet.)

I am released to do many things,
To tile a wall, to make love happily,
To sleep all night, having bright feature dreams
Planning another year, despite Man Friday.

Deeper Than Did Ever Plummet Sound

Why do I wake in the night like this,
Floating to the surface, like a mud bubble?
Was not everything calmed, accepted
As I sank to sleep? Was I not at peace?

The creature that is Caliban or Ariel
In the same island as my rational self,
In the fearsome island of my existence,
Considers not, and tosses me on breakers,
Strands me on the beach of stark beset.

Fearfully I examine my garments for stains,
Am pinched and racked, I hear the ominous noises,
Know my poor self, frightened to the bone
And lie here trying to compose my mind,
Aware of the limitations of my magic.

In The Pyrenées

Nothing at first seemed momentous
As we set off with a bag of mountain ham,
A baguette and goat cheese,
Some nectarines and a bottle of *Pelure d'Oignon*,
Up the path to the church at Sahorre.

So hot the sun on the hillside
I was glad to pause under the dense aspens
In the shadow of the stone – to find
The church a ruin, its walls bulging,
Propped by rough timbers, the windows smashed:
Inside a dim glimpse of a chandelier,
And the graveyard poisoned and sere,
With rusting metal crosses, smashed graves:
But the bell still struck its quarters –
Because someone still climbs to wind the relic.

As so often, in rural France now, the end
Of a way of life, the villages becoming derelict.

So, we go on up, aware of the altitude,
Already two thousand feet, up stony paths,
Glad of the shade when we meet it,
Gloating on the tall blue wildflowers,
The prolific buddleias, the bright butterflies,
Losing ourselves, and then picking up the path.

Suddenly, clear about a thicket
Leaps the Canigou, with its crevasses of ice:
How the mountains move about us as we walk!
Now we climb in fearful confrontation
As the sharp edged peaks climb up into the sky:
We from East Anglia cannot believe it.

A broken-down hamlet called Thorrent
Glows in the heat, with its hay pastures:
Even here are orchards, and dense timber
Where we sit and eat, peering between the trees
At the summer snow on the distant peak.

Is it the air on the height that sets our hearts
Beating back to the thrilling leaps of youth?
You gasp at my absurd proposals
As we roll in the grass of an orchard mead:
The wildflowers wave in the sun at my excesses.

So, we tramp down the road home,
Our little *pension* tantalisingly shifting
Among the woods down in the valley slopes,
Tracing our possession of its configurations
Between the fields of *pommiers* and blue heights
Until we can shut ourselves in the dark bedroom
Wild with the joy and terror of the mountains!

Aspiciens a Longe

I stand waiting outside King's Chapel
For my grandsons to buy their keepsakes:
One comes out with a yellow plastic pen,
The other with a postcard of the Rubens.
I hear people complain of the early darkness,
The December shroud, as the dim lamps are lit.
The ancient stone is eroded black and white
Here and there, and presses into the earth
With the weight of the long and heavy centuries.

I look along the pavement of Gibbs Building:
Have I done enough? What have I done?
Recall the long line of fellows saluting me
Beneath the great daunting God-searching spaces.

Nowadays, I shrug: it is too much to ask
Whether one came up to these magnesite ideals,
One's soul scoured by the great doubts and dauntings:
I grapple at it: recently you were ill,
Lay low in the next room, hearing my silence,
Hour after hour, with the little scratch of the pen:
In the same bed where, in reconciliation, this morning,
We made love, richly, driving the sorrow from our hearts:
That iris in my soul's colour I unroll into the mist
As it falls over the great lawns down to the river.

The dark figures pour out of the stone vaults
As ever: as we gather I remember
Some thin papers I must give the library.

A Death in Spring

To the memory of Peter Burbidge

The middle of May: instead of gathering flowers,
We clip obituaries out of *The Times* –
So thick and fast the deaths: and now
Today I stand in the sunshine in a green graveyard
With a press of sad men in their plain black suits
Beside an open hole, his granddaughters holding posies,
And I kiss the widow's poor torn face.
It is like a scene from Thomas Hardy,
Except for the pain and grief, for they are real.

Instead of going to another memorial service
I forfeit the bright afternoon for an auction sale
In the disused Festival Theatre, where the gods
Are still to be traced above the cyc curve of the stage.
There I am eyed by plastic mannequins,
A severed head, and other thespian properties
While the auctioneers dress up in Augustan costume,
Explode maroons and play naval marches
As they sell marine uniforms and bunting flags.

I feel I am at another funeral, while
The rest of the world has become a farce:
Could we not have had some explosions of confetti
At 'puzzling reflections in a mirror' or 'in short'?
The master undertaker, in a worn top hat,
Seems to be offering 'real coffin handles':
The gauche pop art painting of A GIRL
WHO WANTED LOVE makes as much of an impression
As the ancient tombs I stared at to stem my tears.

A relief when a grey May rain falls,
And we see the evening in a glass darkly.

Queynt

This quaint and generous secret that you keep –
The woman's gift to satisfy us till we sleep
Happily in our bed – how in her graceless face
I come to know the meaning of my universal place!

Yet she is all expressionless and strange, bare
Gateway to being, a triumphant crest of hair
Mockingly curled: her lips display no play
Of fun or sweet embarrassment, or even passion, gay
Though you may be. She, like an unfamiliar growth,
Mussel or limpet, smiles only at ganglion truth
As tides flow in our limbs along strange shores
Where life clings urgently with generation-hungry jaws.
So does she smile, receive him, my awakened, blind,
Eyeless master of her subtle world, whose end
Comes in her warm and cunning comforting embrace.

And if we love in light, so dreadful are our eyes
That we must shut them, only our hands and thighs
Stumbling towards the faceless darkness where we thrall
To achieve our total ransome, to fulfil all.

And while she changes not as I must, simply lies
Close-lipped again, a chafe-blush on your thighs,
Our world is overcome with meaning, and we know
Each other best there, as she tells him, tongueless, he must go.

The Nightmares

They writhe like live things in the night:
Why do they feel like women? They exhaust me,
Baying in cacophonous voices, panicking,
Wrestling with me as I rise and fall
Up to the surface of sleep, or back into their arms.
I have known nights when the clinch of their thighs,
Their blubbering, their palsied yacking
Filled me so full of fear of sleep I lay awake,
Preferring the pain of raggedness of nerve
To treading that sulphurous pit of footless blood.

Though at such times they're seeking to confound me
I can never confront them or arroint them:
They take no shape that can be realised.

There's nothing outwardly wrong with this domestic Sunday:
We are all calm, relaxed, content, indoors,
But my father's widow arrives tomorrow: like a magnet,
Anticipation of the poor sad woman's visit draws them:
Once she is here, they'll join me in mere tears.
But in the night they thrash in uncontrolled
Elaboration of the potential horrors:
On the surface of their shrieking tentacles
Tosses my mother's corpse, my father's ashes,
Torn by earth-shaking thunderclaps and voids
That overwhelm an infant's inexpressible dread
Swollen to fill a man's distensions of despair.

Racked by these vigorous dreads, I stumble,
Rising late, shaking off the cloak of grief and doubt:
Nothing is wrong; no more than a squelchy morning,
As dark as January, and a family day, calm and dull,
Yet so exhausted, I can barely crawl!

Bringing Everything Home

I have to bring my books back from my room:
It is a crisis, everything must move up.
Heavy bundles must be dumped for this.
A world is winding down, temporary
Empty shelves look like the insides of coffins.

Papers fall out, from an old poet friend:
'I must give up this erotic thing,' he says,
'And think of a future life.' I recall
The small confused group of friends
Straggling away from the crematorium.

Here is another hand, firm, regular:
Yesterday his widow gave us lunch.

What's left? The ink-marks on the desk
The books with their edges going brittle,
Cracking and wearing away and splitting.

And who is reading them? At night
In this disappointing July, the rain
Washes out the festival fireworks, we
Scuttle indoors, and in the new houses
The lights of the blue lanterns flicker.

All we can do, sleepy and haunted,
Is to make love, love like great lilies
Briefly blooming in the grey afternoon
Then I shift books still, making room for retirement.

Home Again

Home from hospital, after eight days,
I am afraid of the dark; I dread
Being left alone – after yearning for it
In the terrible ward with its rows of anguish.
There is no red button here, no system
To connect me to the corridors of medical science
Where the specimens fly to the laboratories
To reveal their dreadful truths.

There is only you, wan and tired with love
Even resenting my return a little, grim
With my anxiety and shock. And my dreams,
Of the core exterminator, a metal shell,
Where the essence is refined to nothingness:
Or the flurry of hairy limbs, writhing,
Thudding in some primal vortex in the dark:
I have to have a light on, to prevent me
Sliding into the shadows where these ghosts appear.

In the dawn, I carry out my rigmaroles
While you are still asleep: I am not
Yet awoken enough for the monsters to be human.

A Trip to Vienna

1

We stand on the steps of the Tate Gallery:
Tom is trying to get us a taxi:
Dark sleet clouds blanket the city,
Drenching curtains of rain swirl down on us.
Through the storm an air-liner coasts,
The navigation lights sparkling regularly.
Tomorrow we shall be up there, we think –
You quail at the thought: sodden,
We bundle into the cab, only then
To recall the paintings we have seen –
All rehung, Stanley Spencer's *Cookham*
Churchyard, the gloomy Rothkos, those cables
Enclosing china eggs, the Jackson Pollocks.
Wet and afraid, the boy tired and hungry,
We rattle across Piccadilly, talking
Of the new perspective on British art.

This is an object lesson for us – target the mind
On the continuity of consciousness and culture.

2

After all the apprehension of weeks
A phobia has quit me – I no longer
Fear flying: all those X-ray machines,
Even to see a woman frisked in front of me:
The weigh in, the tickets, even a delay –
I greet the MacDonald Douglas 40,
Sleek, polished and brand new, like an old friend.

At last, we rumble along the runway,
Then I feel the wings take us off, the nose
Lift suddenly, and then, the aisle aslant,
This incredible machine soars up above the clouds,
Where the sunlight breaks in, and below us,
Are the fluffy peaks of rising thermals.

I see the coast of England in no time:
There are little ships making arrowed wakes.
Then we drone above Europe, the air flow
Making my window hiss a little.

Two pretty girls serve us a turkey lunch,
Followed by good Viennese coffee.
Here is the Danube, olive green: we begin
Our descent. The Austrian captain
Tells us we shall experience turbulence,
'But don't worry!'– the plane goes quiet,
The metal wings wobble a little, there
Are a few bumps, and we sink to earth:
You clasp my hand and gasp as we land
And the jets go into noisy reverse action.

After that, the bus to Vienna is boring,
Racing along a freeway lined with immense tanks,
Metal retorts, pipes, a cracking plant:
Our minds are still up there, above the little clouds!

3

How tame Vienna is! The Underground clean,
With neither posters nor barriers, and a taped voice
Snarling 'Karlplatz' and 'Stephanplatz' at us.
The people look docile, dressed in dark clothes,
Many women in fur coats, everyone with fur hats.
We ride out past the Donau Isle, where an oxbow lake
Is set up for swimming, with holiday chalets.

It snows as we walk into the bleak modern building,
Where I talk confusedly to the conference members.

Back in this city, I sit with you for an hour
Over a *melange* in a coffee bar,
Watching it snow heavily, as *fiakers* clop past,
Waiting for our time to collect our tickets
To hear the Vienna Boys' Choir.

It is like a happy dream, with you as a focus:
We two, in love, in Vienna again: how amazing!

4

You are so excited! While I was working
You went to so many elegant shops!
I meet you now as the snow comes on,
As it always does in the late afternoon:
Cold air flows down from the mountains like wine!

I want to show you the Belvedere, yet
I have not eaten – so, we must walk the streets,
Seeking a restaurant I saw up there, with its blackboard.

Our hearts sink, I lose myself, we tramp on,
My blood sugar is low, shall I collapse?
When we reach the auberge, it is firmly closed.
'Oh God!' I cry, and we stagger drunkenly
Towards Prinz Eugene Strasse, wondering what to do.

A couple of lit lamps! A restaurant! Open!
We reel in, and find it a Greek taverna!
After a while, we are drinking dry white wine
Eating a Moussaka whose flavour is exquisite!

How I remember such switches of mood, abroad.
A comic E.M. Forster family from England

Sits next to us with their guidebooks,
Carefully ignoring us, plain and echt Sawston.
But who is that? Fussing at the next table
Alone, is Ed Shils, who shared rooms with me at King's!
He is organising a New European University!
We exchange greetings – but what a coincidence!

Restored, we make our way into the Belvedere
Where, up a corner, as if they were jealous of them,
They show two Renoir nudes, some Cezanne apples,
A Manet boat scene, and two sculptured Eves.

5

Clearly, the best thing about Vienna is eating!
Never mind the Hapsburg crown with its fat jewels
As big as wine gums: the monstrances
Scattering their light about another bit of the True Cross
Or a fragment of some wretched martyr's bones.
Forget even the magnificent heralds' tabards
With their embroidered scutcheons,
The ecclesiastical copes and the bejewelled broadswords.
Never mind that every church you go into
Has a party of devout people praying and whole banks
Of festive candles fixed to the grids.
Forget Canova's tomb for Marie Christine
And the containers of umpteen hearts of the Hapsburgs.

Get in early, deep into the *Augustiner Keller*,
A state eating house, and order a *fiertel*
Of dry white wine, and a grilled pork hock
A half chicken, with a salad, among
Austrian families and lovers, excited and attentive,
In their little niches, devoted to Sunday lunch:
The coffee afterwards is aromatic and rich,
And a great homely benignity overwhelms you!

6

You are wearing your new mustard coat:
We might have posed more elegantly
Had the Stadtpark been a little more springlike.
Vienna is about three weeks behind Cambridge.

We search for a sculpture of Mahler:
I photograph several, the Strauss arch,
The new Bruckner: unfortunately,
I do not remove the lens cap: so, later,
I find them all blanks. Nothing is open yet.
We walk across to the Karlskirche
Past an enormous phallic Henry Moore.
The church interiors are overwhelming:
At first you say, 'Lummee!'
But then they quickly sink to being boring
(There is nothing like Early English to lift the soul).

In an underground cafe, I eat a salad
Sprinkled with lumpfish, then take another snap
Of the Karlskirche through the trees: once again
Still failing to remove the lens cap,
Though the thing went off as I was putting it away,
Taking a perfect picture of Viennese feet and paving!

7

Where else in the world would a publishing director
Who had never met me before in his life,
Invite my wife and me, to his club restaurant,
To make a 'nice foursome', for dinner?
His firm was started by Alma Mahler,
So, we feel in touch with Werfel and those years.
I gave him my poems: he offers us a flat
Whenever we come to Vienna. His wife is Italian,
And we all get on like a house on fire.

He says he thinks English publishing
Has produced too much rubbish, in recent years:
So, he is a man close to my heart!

We sit among the flowers and prints
Enchanted with one another – so intelligent!
His English is so perfect! He drives us home
To our hotel, whence, at five next morning,
We shall begin our journey home. '*Gute nacht!*'
I hope the evening was a success for him, too.

8

We are stacked for a long time
Above the whiter fleecy clouds above London.
If only one had X-ray eyes to see
Some kind of orientation! I don't want to land:
The Alps by Vienna were so mysterious,
White peaks standing above the clouds
Like a strange, wonderfully sculptured city.
For the rest, there was figured clouds below us,
With glimpses of the sea, and a seaport.

Now we just leave it! The plane sinks
Into cloud, into the awful downward transformation:
Below is a grey gloomy day, so dark
One can barely see the fields and houses.
So many cars! So dense the development!

The plane continues to sink – where's the airport?
At last, we are on that long boring tarmac:
It is over, except for a desperate moment
As a woman passenger walks off with your handbag.
Here we are, with it, reclaimed, on the Tube again
Trying to keep our minds on the marvels we have witnessed!

Images of Grieving Woman

The afternoons grow dark, the car lights
Endlessly circulate in meaningless procession:
So often full of darkness and of pain
These tense weeks before Christmas.

This year, your brother's funeral
Takes us over the Welsh border. I do
What I can to help you bear your pain.

Now, a week later, I rise to the surface
On a dark cold morning: as I break
Into consciousness, I see this female figure,
Standing in sadness, her head on one side,
As you stand in your grief, like *Pieta*,
Like so many figures of grieving women,
At the foot of the Cross, or at the Deposition.

The stark forlornness, the silent shadow
of; that figure fills me with such woe
I find it difficult to greet the real woman
Who must stir from a bed of terrible dreams
Into the empty reality of a December morning.

Not Yet, Surely?

The windfall pears fall from the trees –
Not yet surely?
Thudding into the grass in the storm
Lying fat and large in the warm
Last sunshine after: is summer over, then?
Over this year before it has begun!

Pale whitish blue, the frail tips rise –
Not yet surely?
Writhing autumn crocuses, bright
Frail tissues starved of light
Then sinking back to earth: is summer over then?
We have hardly forgotten spring.

A blue fig drops and rolls against my foot –
Not yet surely?
I lift the heavy cloak of darkening shrouds:
The tree is heavy with its pulpy loads
Yearning for mouths: is summer over, then?
Let us enjoy the rich flesh while we can!

A Death

Another death in the newspaper columns:
You are shattered by the loss of an old friend,
A woman you hadn't seen for years:
'I felt sure', you say, 'I would see her name';
We go over the few occasions when we met her.

Every now and then one catches a glimpse
Of the water pouring over the weir:
Figures flash down more and more often, and sink
Without time to say goodbye or make amends.
Events we shared, like D-Day or the 1945 Election,
Take on a new distorted character:
The firm record of memory is eroded,
Replaced by falsifications and substitutions:
One is left with a terror of relinquishing
The memories that are one's life.

So, we walk out, silent, along the river
And every now and then your hand creeps
Feeble and sad, into mine: this light touch
Holds us above the surface of black despair.
But the day is good, a first day of summer,
And we cling to the occasional caress of a bright sun
Hardly daring to look one another in the face.

Verona

The outer walls of the Roman arena
Soar blackly into the sky, and beneath
The huge dark tunnels loom:
The horror of blood, savagery and sick indulgence,
Crowds gloating on death and pain.

Today the arena is being fitted out
For a performance of Bellini's *Norma*,
A massive operatic picnic: gelati fridges
Are wired in every section; yet on a pole
I find a sticker saying, 'I love my dentist.'

The immense stone erection devoted
To brutal voyeurism leaves us stunned:
We feel happier in the charming Piazza delle Erbe
Where the market stalls are set out with colourful native
                                                taste
Under the facades of distinguished buildings.
So, we progress into the Piazza dei Signori.
Beneath the council loggia, in a high-class restaurant
Where the clientele wear suits and the waiters cringe:
We dare not even read the menu, because of its rows of
                                                noughts,
And turn to the rival place, where families
With little children are eating, and where
For a mere ten pounds we have ravioli, with egg sauce,
Salad and wine: Trattoria 'Impero',
By a statue of someone who looks like Dante,
All splashed with pigeon muck,
And absorb the strange mixture of Roman and mediaeval
Before I go off to paint the Ponte di Pietra,
The ancient Roman bridge that spans the Adige,
Where the water leaps like little dolphins!

Changing the Scene

Eight o'clock on a Saturday morning:
No one in the streets but two monks and
A nervous policeman: I pause by the gap
In the fence beyond David's bookshop,
Gaze into the workings for the new Arts Theatre.

A mechanical digger has been scraping away,
Filling steel tubs with rubble, to be
Lifted by the crane that towers over the site.
There are some rickety old walls marked 'RETAIN'.
The rest has gone, leaving a wounded vacancy
In which I can see the marks of mirrors
Surrounded by bulb holders, in a row:
Can those really have been the dressing-rooms,
Down there, almost level with the sewers?
Was it from there the elegant Chekov women,
Shakespeare's fairies and the pantomime dames
Emerged, to climb the stairs, to the space of the stage?
There was the prop room, and above the chasm
The fly platform where my sons heaved at the tackle
And cut their names in the wall that has now fallen.

Will they ever reconstruct this playhouse
To recreate the Thespian illusions
Such as used to hold our children spellbound?
Those diaphanous figures in a blue light
Dancing behind a gauze with an electric moon?
Bricks and earth, bars of steel, breeze-blocks
Lie higgledy-piggledy in a vast hole:
I cannot make any sense of it yet!

If only, in the present state of things one could hope
For a transported moment – a Venetian street

A wood near Athens, the Forest of Arden,
Where a woman's figure might draw one's soul into a rapture.
Alas, all this constructive effort for a show
Is likely to be a platform for endless contempt
As mundane as this heap of spoil and metal rubbish,
I say, pulling my head back in despair.

Art and Life

I spend a weekend mending cracks in the walls:
Those white unbroken surfaces are so satisfying!
I also cook *Coquilles de Turbot au Gratin*,
Dig out a few wild buttercups, make love to you,
Have a crisis over my estimation of Tolstoy:
(Perhaps all that search for meaning through woman,
Is self-deception, bunkum, really, I think?)

A composer friend rings up out of the blue,
Talks about living in France, where, he says,
They respect the artist: his bank manager
Virtually went down on his knees to him
When he found he was a composer of music.
Here, we agreed, most of the stuff in the press
Is dead: next month, I tell him, I bring out another novel
That will sink into the indifferent silence.
Its a strange world, I tell him, like one of those dreams
In which one tries to speak, and no sound
Can emerge from your lips.

       So, why not
Escape from it by mixing up plaster,
Mending the cracks in the walls, and cooking
Delicious meals, where the happiness lies
Between delicate glasses of an Australian Semillon
And a slice of Chaource cheese, just at ripeness?

Belonging

A distant funeral leaves us a sense of loss,
Associated with a view of Stonehenge at sunset:
Never again will that quirky colleague
Make us laugh, or surprise us by his phrases.

During the night, the same week, a burglar
Forces his way in, goes out with our teapoy,
One of the first things that we bought together.

The children miss it more than we do,
They remember how hard it was to lift the lid
With their little fingers; and the ancient scent
Of secret tea compartments
Lined with lead: we never kept anything in it
But the smell of centuries hung on in there
And in their memories. My dreams
Are full of mysterious lost caskets
In which old memories of valueless things
Cling in the face of obsessive removal.

Soon, surely, we shall have nothing left
Except the faintest breathings of the past
That once gave joy, and a sense of belonging?

Original Sin

Ella Constance, aged two, comes to lunch
With her father, my son, and her sister Zoë.
I am cleaning up afterwards in the kitchen
And I hear this little maid fumbling
At the key of the downstairs lavatory,
Trying to lock herself in, in modesty.
Later, she finds her tiny fingers too tender
To turn the key the other way, to let herself out.

There is no outside keyhole, we cannot attack
The door from the outside: the window
Has had locks put on it, after the latest
Burglary: so, what are we to do?
Little old Ella is locked in the lavatory!
We try to urge her to tackle the lock again
But she becomes hysterical, lies down
Beside the pan in a paroxysm of rage.
Her father tries to calm her down, her sister
Reasons with her: we all stand round urging
The child to remain reasonable, but, alas,
She has no resources left to gain self-command.

At last, with a spade, I heave up the sash
Until the catch breaks and the window jams
Against the new locks and my practical son
Thrusts in his arm and unlocks the door!

A pale, frightened, sobbing child is lifted and hugged:
Not used to this sort of thing, I watch her
Gingerly, as she bumps about the kitchen,
Totters along the path by the river, wades
In her wellington boots through huge puddles.
And when we return to the garden afterwards

Deliberately stamps on a group of daffodil spears,
Then soars away into a storm of tears.
There is outcry, but I laugh, though I'm also alarmed
At such a demonstration of original sin.

Late August

It is a shock, the way parts of this house
Are sinking, cracking the plaster:
You can see through some of the walls!
How familiar, these damp patches here and there,
The impulse to strip off the encroaching ivy,
To clear the gutters, to thrust one's hand
Into a silted drain and flush it free:
I have been doing it, sporadically,
For nearly half a century. The rains
Do not relent, the sun goes on burning,
Shrinking the clay so that the house leans over.

Like Noah and his wife, we go on sailing
Through the years, making our meals,
Making love, sewing pillowcases, reading:
Sometimes we hit highs, sometimes disappointments
Not of our making, but from some inner ghost
Or simply the natural cycles of the pathogens,
The darting of the dragonflies, or wasps,
Or the sudden pelting flurry of a shower,
As one now tosses the trees and drums on the windows
And I rush out to warn you to get the washing in:
But, your dear head calm, you go on ironing
Resigned, as I am, to simply let it pass.

From a Back Window

So hot, we have to devise new tactics,
To keep in a shadow, or draw the curtains.
So, I am sitting by a back room window
Where a gentle breeze is blissfully touching me.

I gaze at a brick wall, thinking
This is not very poetic, until I notice
How the matching of cream and pink and grey
Speaks of a man's intuition, while the mortar
Seals the motion of his hands in its set
Smears and ridges, with a blue patch
Here, and then a dark peacock butterfly
Comes and completes the picture,

Whose beauty in the quotidian makes me think of you,
So long the companion of my life, and like
The saving gift of a cold bubbling spring
Found among rocks half way up a mountain
To sooth my parched long drawn out misery;
Or like a field of tall flowers
Suddenly come upon, on a summer walk,
A gift of glad life, to a dry and weary soul.

So it is, often, that we find in daily life,
As when we glance at one another and know
At once what the other is thinking,
In gratitude at the gift of love
That surprises us in the most unlikely settings.

The New Member Tries to Sit Up

Waking, she sees her grandmother,
Stares, ponders, then in gleeful recognition,
Chortles and smiles. Of course, we dance,
Startling the creature out of her wits.
It takes some time, and a great deal of thought
For her to calm down, and we, ashamed,
Try to remember what it is like to be
Only four months old, when the world
Is not yet put together, nor the self.

And then, seized with a fresh desire
To view the world and the people, Anna
Arches her back, tries to lift herself
Into the sitting posture, bravely arches,
Then gives it up, and with her lower lip
Expresses disappointment.'Oh, not yet,
Not yet,' we say.'Soon Anna will sit up!'

Can you believe there was a time when we
Couldn't sit up? And it required such
Courage to fling oneself, into that mode,
And then to hump one's way about the floor,
At last to stand! One day this mite will rise
And enter on her long perambulation –
But, for the moment, sinks down, lies resigned!

A Weekend in Bruges

In the Burg, the main square of Bruges,
A party of Belgian WRNS cheers and cries,
Releasing hundreds of blue balloons that soar away
Over the cakey renaissance Landhuis.
There is a smell of horsepiss from the fiakers
While crowds of sightseers push or queue
As we walk through to the Vismarkt.

What can hold all these excitements together,
The beautiful paintings of dreadful events,
A man being skinned alive, another being eaten
By a devil, another cut in two by a huge knife
Courtesy of Hieronymous Bosch? Baguettes
Of chewy Belgian bread and Brie and ham
Fortify us for our tramp over the endless pavé
And a love-in in the hotel bedroom
Where the canals meet, and the waterboats
Continually chug past packed with tourists?

Nothing brings it all together: how can we
Adopt the meaning systems of the Middle Ages:
All we can do is to savour the empty shells
Of the lovely houses and the burgers'.palaces
In a world that has only a frenetic impulse
To taste everything and scrutinise it, without commitment?

Oxford, In the Sheldonian Theatre

We look down from the galleries of the theatre:
The ceiling is painted with a vast symbolic scene –
Learning of various kinds defeating Envy and Ignorance –
Too elaborate to take in, while, below,
Dons in red robes mumble their Latin and bow,
Walk to and fro and touch their students
On their heads in fours with the Holy Book.
Cameras flash, and you can hear every language.
The supplicants or whatever you call them
All go out, then come in with their robes on
To applause: two babies are taken out
To stop them wrecking the solemn atmosphere.
Our young friend is among the hallowed throng:
Now members of his college may call him 'Doctor'.
Meanwhile the university is hard up, every year
Students are less well read, standards are slipping,
We have the Kellogg College and the Rupert Murdoch
Professor of Communication and Media Studies.
Strange things are going on in the name of Physics,
Chemical and Molecular manipulations,
Based on the need to exploit, for profit,
What is left of the ecosphere, mineral resources,
Fossil energy, while the forests are destroyed.
Can God hold it all together any longer?
Certainly the mumbling Latin carries no conviction.
Shall we look to the ancient world for wisdom?
Or where shall wisdom be found?
The funny hats and gowns are returned to the shops:
Everyone is pleased as they snap one another
Among the hefty stone architectural porticos
Before they off to take tea and toasted muffins,
Then try to find their way home in the exasperating traffic
Jammed nose to tail along the High
Where, I note, they charge a pound to go into Balliol.

Moony

We pull off the motorway to the Ashwell road,
Stop in the dark, in a field, to catch
The new moon, one horn hanging in a cloud
Before it sinks into the sunset. Quick!
Get hold of your shilling before it goes!
So, in the dark out on the road you bow quickly, gentle,
Pretty, superstitious, Welsh and silly,
My woman, telling me, 'What! Just before
We go on an aeroplane, not to do the new moon?'

June Again

Once again, it is early June, and my funk
Grips me, my D-Day apprehension –
Worse this year, as I have to attend a reunion.

Peonies and delphiniums splash the border
Of the neat garden of Hall Place, where Ted,
The adjutant who was with me in the bombardment
Is talking to Whitty, who put me in the ambulance.

It is a better day than was promised
And we set to, to the wine and the pretty salads,
Still wondering why we have come.

Here is Ernest, and Alan Thornton and Norman:
We forget the forty-six years that have passed,
Get into a huddle, and re-create the amazing
Events we were caught up in, as little more than boys,
Sounding a little like Dogberry – but the sons here
Sit with their eyes popping, hearing stories
No-one has ever told before. Here is Mitchell,
Blown out of a tank turret to lie
Unconscious for four days, a blackened spectacle,
Now, it seems, without a mark on him: Paul,
Who was blinded by a shell, but now can see,
Except that he can no longer tolerate snow.

I am relieved to find I was the *enfant*
Terrible, of those days: though I passed:
I learn that our regiment was considered
'Expendable', in the forward planning.

We compress two years driving to the edge
Of endurance, into one sunny hour, then leave

37

In a happy frame of mind, contented
To remind ourselves that it really happened:
Escaping death by a hair many times a day,
Doing what we could for the wounded, hoping
We would survive: which we did – otherwise
I would never have known you, would never have written
A word, would have lain in one of those
Neat graveyards, like Douvres la Delivrande,
With no one left by now to mourn me!

An Episode

I stand in the living room of a terrace house,
Water pouring down through the ceiling above me,
Dripping on my face: the frost has broken
Pipes in the attic, and the whole place
Is swamped with flood. It is your house,
Your little house you bought with a legacy
From your mother, and you bind it up
With all your love and hope for the future.

Now it is full of strangers: a fire officer
Is poking a screwdriver through the plaster
To relieve the flood, so that the weight of water
Doesn't bring the ceilings down: buckets and pans
Stand everywhere, musically dripping. Upstairs,
The bed is soaked, the carpets are sodden.

A dreamlike detachment overcomes me:
I wander up and down the stairs, getting
Into everybody's way: I try to consider
What I could do, then decide I can do nothing.

At last, I go home to fetch some bowls,
Collect you, so now you stand here too
In this indoor storm, sobbing and desolate;
It is a common catastrophe, they tell us, this week.

All night the awfulness of it haunts us:
Your heart behaves in a stressful way, you say.
Gradually, I reassure you and myself that
Nothing has happened that money can't put right:
It is not the death that it first seems –
Merely a domestic event, a mere episode.

Old Photographs

Part of the mythology of our life
These glimpses of Wales in old photos,
The Garth Mountain, and the brick urinal
On the corner opposite, the walnut tree
At several stages of growth, and the garden seat.

There's you, at two or three, on your tricycle
Or sitting plump with a grin between two
Big ears; posturing with a sunshade,
Or lounging on a rock with your brother.

The photos are going curled and faded,
The brother is dead with the rest of them:
We'll never go near the place again.

I gloat on the curves of your young hips,
On the plump breasts of your adolescence:
Now, I have enjoyed you for many decades.
I feel a tender poignancy for the long sticks
Of the legs of these figures at that stage
Between childhood and maturity, where the form
Writhes with uncertainty as to who it is.

I feel the same of myself, at that time:
From the fading pictures I catch that sometime dread
About the future, and there you are
With X and Y and God knows who – at last
I married you, and everything else unfolds
Through umpteen well-thumbed family albums.

Only, where is it now, that all the subjects
Are no longer in the world, only in our minds
And some of the shadows we cannot even remember

Or have lost all contact with, or have gone:
What did we keep this detritis for
Unless to prove that the eventual substance
Was so much richer than the original sketch-plan?

Two Canvasses

I brought two blank canvasses back from France:
Never, once there, was there one of those moments
Of abandonment, to the joy of fixing
Some aspect of that happy country in paint.

So, I am guilty, and in the middle of July
A hot wind blows, dust from a volcano
(Mount Pinatubo) blights the world's season:
But there are good days when the sun shines.

I seize one of them, wheel my stuff across
Midsummer Common, to the riverside,
And paint the footbridge with the dark trees
Where the dense shadows hold them firmly
Against the bright sunshine in the warm wind.
I struggle with a bright swept water surface.

What satisfaction, when the thing comes off!
Quite lost in the effort, abandoned
To a skill I cannot summon or control:
It only happens, and one can't say why.

And now it seizes me again – almost
Before I'm awake, I decide to try
The picture I have seen a thousand times
Coming out of P staircase from my college room.

All next day I sweat at it: it must be done
Carefully. People come by and twig me:
I sweep the cirrus flecks across the sky:
I get the ridges of the buildings right.

At last it is done, that orderly scene
That transforms the sky above the level roofs
Into the painted sky of an eighteenth century landscape.
As I work on the final detail, what it says
Is 'In pursuit of the ideals we cannot
Ever achieve': when it is dry
I shall show it in college: will anyone
See from the picture that I meant it so?

Next day, I feel as if I have been drunk,
Exhausted by being in the wild grip of summer,
But glad to have given myself into its reckless hands!

The Flotilla

'The Last Fling', The Sun', 'The Iron Maiden'–
The houseboats all have rakish names,
Stretching from Midsummer to Stourbridge Common.
We walk all along them, this August afternoon.

Some are freshly painted, with flowers in boxes,
Red and white geraniums, windmills and kittens:
Little piles of logs to feed their smoking stoves.
These are the successful ones, thriving households.
But others are listing, filling with water,
Their plywood peeling and rotting, sinking:
One can see from the thrown down paintbrushes
Their owners have been striving, but, at last,
Have given up and abandoned them to decay.

How like my own enterprises, I think!
Some of them now sadly beyond ever being shipshape.
I remember hammering and planing, filling
The cracks in the plywood with Bostik:
We punted and rowed, or borrowed an outboard,
Navigated between banks of nettles,
Until the planks gave way and let the water in:
In the end, I sawed them up and dumped them.

Now, some of my writings seem likely
To go at last, in the same way,
As a similar neglect overtakes us, and ennui:
What seemed at first a thrilling adventurous
Way of life becomes dull and awkward:
As the autumn sets in, the fabric
Becomes leaky and expensive, one's spirit
Grows distrustful, timid and intolerant:

Coming back, I'm prepared to let half of them go!

Number Seven

I hold my seventh grandchild,
A new scrap of life, nine months old:
She hollers so loudly my left ear goes deaf,
Then, after a while, looks at me so steadily,
Without a blink, under her exquisite eye lashes,
She seems to be looking into my soul.

That scrutiny makes me uncomfortable,
But, fortunately, she can't speak yet.
However, it is clear she has a will,
Knows exactly what she wants, not only
Cake or milk, but to go on swimming,
Held up only by an inflatable ring,
Bravely getting swamped and coming up again,
Grinning all over her face: so self-
Possessed, I foresee her dealing with a lover:
Enjoying him with delicious abandon,
Inspiring him to incredible adventures!

How she takes hold of the world
I think, watching her with her mother
And sister, playing Ring-a-ring-a-roses
In the water of the pool, then, almost at once,
Going to sleep on her father's knee.

Such charm! Such deliberateness!
Such self-possession! – I give up thinking
Ours is a terrible world – how can it be,
With such promising creatures in it
As Ella Constance, who so likes waving
At me, in recognition, mind to mind!

Bowels

'Don't move!' 'Don't breathe!', he cries,
The radiography doctor: so, I pose
In twenty postures, on his huge machine.

Suddenly, I catch sight, in a bright tank,
Of a convoluted creature, primaeval,
Trembling with life, in a blue light,
Shivering tenderly, like a sea anemone,
Or a sensitive octopus, on his screen.

With a pang, I realise, it is my bowels,
Leading their other life, as organism,
Suffering under the excruciating violation
Of medical examination: unfamiliar,
Indeed, utterly other, belonging
To that life that goes on within one's body
Following the patterns and rhythms of the earth.

I get dressed and go out, hoping that nothing
Is wrong: followed by that ghostly image
Of the polyp that is me and not me,
Lying at the bottom of my internal sea,
Winding and writhing under my compassions.

The Cemetery

What an extraordinary occupation for a holiday!
Here in the *Cimitière de Monmartre*
Are suddenly Heinrich Heine, in white stone,
Zola, Balzac, Stendhal – all in their hollow cupboards,
Family tombs, with fresh flowers on some of them.
Maigre old ladies and young girls sitting here
Tense with the distinction between hot sun
And the ghastly *objets funaires, 'en perpetuité.'*

Despite the great traffic bridge violating it,
It is charming, with that true Parisian bourgeois
Sense of its own multifarious culture.
As the black attendant rang the closing bell
I puzzled over the family tomb of Sacha Guitry
And his film image flickered faintly in my mind:
I try to remember whether he was a good or bad thing?
In the finality of this place, what does it matter?

Grief

Our little yard looks grim – the plants
Have come indoors, for fear of a frost:
Winter is coming fast, and the dark falls early.
We have a crisis in the small hours.
I am full of fear: I challenge you
After our loving went a little wrong,
Only to be met by the affirmation
'I love you!' and you say
'I do not know what storm was in my soul.'

★

Beneath our familiar ease, a chilly finger
Lays itself on your lips, beyond my word or kiss.
What is happening to us? Later, as we lie talking
You say 'What does it matter? What does any of it matter?'

★

It was like a moment in music
When towards the end of a long conflict
You hear an unexpected note
That resolves everything:
We went to sleep, holding one another.
My head was in her hands, she slept.

I awoke and felt her hands pulsing
Slightly, making soft movements, as if
Caressing someone in a dream.

★

I shall never know
What the grief was. I could only
Try to guess what had impelled her,
Sleeping, to work her hands so
Slightly, in care and love,
Unravelling the cruel world,
Giving me a taste of another realm
She was experiencing in her sleeping mind.

★

All I could do was to be present and patient!
Marvellous courageous dreams she had –
About 'King Asyouweros' – I laughed at them.
Her psyche struggled with its shadows, then
With a glad step, whistling in the kitchen,
Here you are, with me, love, again!

★

Suddenly, coming out of the Tropical House,
We came across a plant in the corridor
We'd never seen in flower before,
Hanging a myriad of long white tubes
Like pure purses, swollen and open,
Attached to each branch with a soft fluffy finger:
So delicate, so charming and so fertile,
They wait for some huge moth or humming bird
To engender their fulfilment. Their perfect
Cheek-like curves tell us we have come through.

The Trick of Light

The gentle sunlight melting through the trees:
I see it on the hill in St Emilion,
Walking past the Old Convent – must go fetch
My paints, and try to capture this light magic:
Nearly do, bring it home and work on it:
In the end I get it right, after a struggle!

Now, as I sit here, I note the same sun
Sinking over Cambridge, is doing just that,
Goldening the willow opposite my window
As it turns yellow-grey – out there,
In *la grande chaleur exceptionelle*,
That touch of lingering sunlight was a touch of home!

Picking up a Scrap of Newspaper from a Fire

'I WAS TOLD WE WEREN'T GOING TO MAKE IT,'
SAYS PRETTY BELINDA.
I spike the page on a nail on the fence.
The loppings are beginning to seethe:
All that wood the children dragged in
Has been piled here, sodden, all the winter.
Now the earth is like piecrust, collapsing,
After the thaw, and the snowdrops clear their fangs,
I celebrate the season with a bonfire. The boys
Bring newspaper and straw: at last
I see the true quick tongues of lilac flame.

Pretty Belinda smiles at the photographer, still human.
At the enquiry she spoke white-faced of her ordeal.
She was thrown clear of the aircraft: earlier
A steward had told her, 'We're not going to get in.'
'He was a nervy type: he died as we struck the houses.'

There is a crisis in the bonfire, packed limbs crack,
A vortex roars. I recognise some of the logs,
An old plum, gale-torn elm-crooks, exploding yew.
The ash fluffs and whitens: a real holocaust down there.

From where she lay Belinda, helpless, heard
A woman say, 'I am burning.' Another, 'Help!'
'I can't get my belt undone!' — then
'A tremendous explosion blew the rescuers back.'

I crumple up Belinda and she flashes in the fire.
A black thin rag of ash soars away over the barn
Twinkling with small red stars. I try to keep my thoughts
Sane for Tom's sake, who holds my hand:
But inwardly I am mad, remembering fiery stars

Passing me, as close as this fire: I hear burning men
Shout from their tanks again, their tissues rising,
A long ghostly column of scintillating gas
Lashing towards the sky: and superb contentment
I feel, because I am unscathed, a finger length from death.

But why should I escape, to hold a love-child's hand?
I wonder if pretty Belinda ever wonders
How the bloom-thin skin of now, so real and peaceful,
But masks the dreadful that has already happened?

June Air Display

Ten men are falling from the clouds,
Blue smoke pouring from their feet.
Up away in the wood across the green corn
You call 'Coo-ee!' and I see your brown figure.

You don't see me, or the parachutists.
(Remember one day, somewhere in France
A man hurtled from the sky in harness?)
On D-Day I must have seen two thousand.

Miles of June green, and the blue woods:
I sit alone, watching the distant air display,
More interested in the larks that soar and sing
Their evocative wheeling song and flutter down
At the edge of the beans in flower, to earth.

Such old memories: piston aircraft in the clouds:
And then me telling the children, at such shows;
You, having heard everything, now so blasé
You don't even see a real free drop of men
Falling a thousand feet in a great smoky spiral!
When the wind rustles in the new green corn,
The larks sing, and the aircraft scour the silence
I hear the ghosts of boys and men pass by
So long dead, they are as ancient as the larks' song.

At home, your thimble, bright and worn, on a tray:
The roses about to come out; field-vetch
Twined in a wildflower bouquet in your room.
Ah, the good years, the blessed benefit,
That I was missed, that I, by an inch, survived!

Now you, miniscule brown figure on Little Trees Hill
Across the wheatfield, two hedgerows away
Didn't even see the Devils falling from the sky!
Nor me, sitting on a red car, in the great green landscape!

After Visiting The Pompeii Exhibition

'What is it?' you say to yourself,
After a long wait in the rain in the courtyard
Shuffling forward with the crowd under an awning.
It is a girl, lying down, in plaster,
Her scanty clothes wreathing her lightly,
Her hair with a soft curl in it
Gathered into a loose bun,
One or two strands straying as she fell.

Ash all the morning, ash all the afternoon:
A glass column shows how ten feet high
White cinders buried her, after the first fallout.

They pumped liquid plaster of Paris
Into the hole that was her: so,
We have her form, her prostration.

The silver drinking cups, the necklaces,
The *lares* and the weighing devices
Seem so domestic and familiar:
Carved masks and portrait busts in stone
So full of confidence and vitality.
Bold sweeps of bronze folds in a black statue,
Maximillius making a public gesture:
How well one knows that Roman signature
Upon the world, upon our consciousness.

But she is something new, or, rather,
The imprint of this girl-shaped hole in ash is:
Her gown pulled up like my woman's nightdress;
The movement of her subjection to fire,
The flower of her body, held there
Quite without morbidity, lithe and slender
As she was, the day before the end of the world.

Hardy Country

I am reading a book called *Life After Death*:
You are strumming your way through hymns
On our scholar friend's piano, whose books daunt me,
Range after range, on philosophy and meaning.
Grey-green, the trees shiver in the cold:
Another August gale is promised tomorrow.

This is a holiday in England, this damp
Stretch of nettles and mud, where the flies bite,
The rills dribble the shaly paths, the air
Is loaded with Atlantic heaviness, and clouds
Heave up towards the moors, stifling us.

Yesterday, almost to the date, we followed
Thomas Hardy and Emma up the Valency path,
A hundred and nine years later. The clearings
Were full of butterflies. And up on Beeny
We sat in a brief sun-spell, drinking wine,
Dizzy with the gulls over the chasms, the cliff
Black and the tail end of a great gale spuming.

And there you are, playing hymns, and I love you,
Among the grey shivering leaves, and the drizzle
Falling all day, this bad summer. Smoke
Drifts through the hedge from a neighbour's bonfire
And we do nothing: there is no drama:
I do not even catch a trout in the stream.

What shall we remember, in our old diaries?

Perhaps the sequence of gales, and the one moment
In Hardy's footsteps, over the jewel coloured sea,
Grass green and blue, below us in Pentargan Bay?

Games We Play

This is one of the games we play:
You are puzzled about what to wear
On some occasion that's coming to pass.
I cannot care as you do, but I watch,
Lying on the bed, you, stripped to your briefs,
Rummaging in the cupboards, flouncing silks,
Skirts with tapes, frocks with laces and slits
As though you were fifty species of flower:
Brick reds and purples, white broderie,
Long pale garments, stripey sleeves that balloon.

You love to be looked at, in such a mood:
I pay you tributes all the time.
We never solve the problem: a gesture
Will arrange the right petals at the moment.

But we share a journey through time –
Second-hand discoveries, new things,
Bought for a trip around the world, frocks
That have never quite come off:
Others that have gone into our legends.

You are content with so little! I want
To buy you armfuls of hissing silks,
Set you out in astonishments, like our
Amazing amaryllis, or the white jasmine
Bursting out this late winter moment.

Alas, my pocket is not equal to my love:
I love you in your old contrivances
Putting this well-known delight with that:
I can only dream of possibilities
Now sliding forever away from us, as

We drift down time, as the garments wear
For all your assiduous attention to their seams
With your mouth full of pins, and me
Admiring your pantomime in the intimate bedroom.

Open Day at Our Old Village

I sit on a wooden see-saw in a country garden,
My grand-children scuttling about among the cowslips
Disobeying and growling at one another
And a fair-haired four-year-old called Tabitha:
Me in a conflict of dimensions,
The great May meadow spaces that I love
Between the beech woods and the Brewery wall
And high above them the immense towers leaning
Over of early summer storm clouds and their
Grey curtains of rain drawing across the West:

Now and familiar the soaked swards of grass,
But under my feet the precipitous vacancies
Like the air space under the eternal rill
Of forceful water streaming down the Mill:
Face after face and figure after figure
That I knew here, and which are nothing now,
Meadow and lanes like a wide splendid stage
With more than half the characters exeunt.

Inevitably, revisiting the village, we hear more
Of those who have gone, or seem to be on their way:
And I think, as I press my stick in the sodden turf,
Of the poetry I teach, or a glimpse of another world,
Or wrestling with God, or cadences of prayer:
There is no one to wrestle with; there is no one there:
A comet rushing towards the earth, rain blight,
This April and May spoiled by sombre skies
And nothing to believe in, only the kingcup bunch
Trembling beneath the sluice-gate, and the petals
Clinging to the bare wet feet of children
Tumbling and swinging in their babbling play.

Thoth and an Aura

I am meeting a philosopher in 'The Bunghole',
A wine bar in High Holborn, but I have an hour
Between the distressed arches of Liverpool Street
And Bloomsbury Square, where I flavour the name
For its aftertaste of snobbery and voyeurism.

So, I cross the forecourt of the British Museum
With crocodiles of Danes and Japanese,
The architrave pressing heavily on the morning.

At the entrance, I have to exhibit my books
To a uniformed man, to show they are not bombs.

All the week, my students have chewed the fat
Around signifiers, referents, and concepts:
I enter the temple sardonic about meanings
Having changed carriages in the Tube train
Because of an unattended package, only
To have confirmed, by the search of my bag
That there is an absence among us, of the fanatic,
The cold bowel tearing maniac with a hate-idea in his head.

Thus I am glad to see Augustus turning, bust by bust,
From his windswept self into a pious god.

But then the great stone arms overwhelm me
In the new Egyptian gallery: red boulders
Carved into elephantine heads with cruel lips,
Sphinxes and lion-headed monsters, guarding
Empty unused sarcophaguses, later used as baths.

It is all a joke, I find, the mausoleums
Chipped with hieroglyphics or wedge writing,

Incomprehensible cuneiform runes – all telling
About forgotten skirmishes over patches of scrub.
A whole great room, given to house size carvings
All showing soldiers carrying bearded heads,
Having them counted by scribes: disgust
Sickens me, that I belong to the same species.

King Shabaha found a slab of black basalt,
Had on it inscribed the history of the world,
How Ptah created all, in white letters
So that the legend should be preserved for Eternity:
Someone had turned it into a useful millstone,
The ridges starring and scarring the Lexicon.

Thoth! Sennacherib! Well, the blood flowed,
The wedges and chisels wrote it up:
The fat strutting ones perished and stank:
Lumps of waste: and power signs fill the galleries,
Most of them tiresome monuments to meanness.

Until I come to three Greek girls in chitons
Stone carved into muslin folds over their bodies
Flowing like bubbling water over their breasts and pubic mounds:
Nereids or auras, personified breezes.
I fell in love at once with the third little gust on the right
Sprung from a consciousness of joy in limbfold,
Lightness in the sunshine and the air of spring.

I took her out in my soul, knowing her
Safe in the confident neo-classical atrium
Until I visit her again: no one searched me.

Erithacus Rubecula

Familiar spirit, in my town garden,
Whistles the robin's winter song
Aware that I am disturbing the fallen colour
Where, below, he will find food in the earth,
Writhing specks too small for me to read.

So, this scrap hooks his talons on the edge,
My galvanised metal barrow: I hear
The scrape of his nail: and as I watch
The wind lifts the thin grey fluff-down
And a shiver goes over his breast like a wave.

I stand for a moment chilled inside the knot
Of his ganglia and entrails, under the quills:
He whistles with energy he can barely spare
From the grub seeking work to fill a miniscule gizzard.

Common and taken for granted, yet
This touch of stuff relates to me strongly,
'Joins' me, and, in response to my machines,
Discriminates between the benign and the annoying:
He dislikes my leaf-sweeper, because of its nasty noise.
They write books on him, in zoo studies.

As I begin to rake again, I know it cannot be
That this autonomous handful could have come into existence
By chance mutations and selecting out: I know it,
It is inconceivable – his trills tell of an intelligence
Determined to have him in this world, as he is:

Startled at the thought, I board up the fall
Into my sacks, and look at my hands, filthy
Among the scarlet and black: how shall we formulate this
Restoring the evident mystery of formation
To a world made bleak by blind mechanics
That can explain nothing: as, eyeing me, the redbreast sings?

The Auction

Your arm seemed rather thin, as I remember it,
Pale and vulnerable, in the cotton sleeve:
So quickly after we met, we grew conspiratorial
From what then grew between us in our glances.

Soon, I was at that house in Wales, your home:
Primroses grew in the unkempt lawns, yellow
Lichen on the stone walls, two small mountains
Each side of the valley. The interiors 'pre-war',
With an air of time having dropped everything
And no man about the house: unmended,
In decline, ruled by your mother's will
About the taps, the water pressure and the smoky hearth.

Yesterday, everything went – the dull chairs,
The imitation flame electric fire, the law books,
Huge mahogany wardrobes grunted down the stairs,
The hideous carved stools, the bad watercolours.

Did we ever make love in the house? It shrank
Our libido: yet I was touched by your joy
In old photographs, or your Daddy's cuff links,
Or the lace shawls and seedy furs in the chest.

Never again shall we go there, Trefaldwyn,
Its windows and panels smashed by thieves,
The paper peeling from its ceilings: I,
The son-in-law, close with its brass latch
Thirty-five years of loving you, fifty
Pages in the family album, the chubby figure
Of a girl of two that was you, the ghost
Father, the poplars and pears and walnuts
All died long ago, with the rusty garden swing.

Blackberrying in the Lane, and, yes, making love in the bracken
On Bedwas Mountain, high up above the Pit.

The Problem of Woman in Oxford

A grey cold April persists: Oxford
Daunts us, with its massive square-cut walls
Weighing with confident reason on the spirit:
In Merton Library the floor sank under the weight,
Ponderous polished planks, huge tomes in ranks:
We thumb through handsome print on unfaded paper.

The mind sails through the centuries, accumulating.
We, transient as the grey-green algae shadow on the stones,
Flit through the courts, missing one another.
Outside the guest room, high above Mob Court,
The tilers hammer and play their transistors.

I hardly speak to you, my face in pain
With a simple cold sore, and stage fright.
At last I raise myself to give a lecture
On the Phantom Woman of the Unconscious.
One of those coldly beautiful women students
Comes up and talks to me about the positive image
Of the female genital, dressed in severe black.

I imagine raising the subject in the breakfast room
Where the silent fellows do not speak to us.

Outside the thick walls, I notice how the frost
Has cut so many pocks in the ochre fabric,
As if the great place were sinking, with Duns Scotus'
Ghost walking on his knees between the Theology,
Meeting T.S. Eliot, browned by his refining fire,
On the upper level. There are no ghosts –
My umbrella, our baggage and our parking tickets
Are real, and the mind's effective priority
Is to delineate the beautiful structure of Herpes simplex:

But all the same, I have a sense of triumph
At having introduced the Problem of the Witch,
Who inhabits us all, as much as our antigens,
Into the heart of the Other Place.

Am I a Sort of Sorabji?

Sometimes the chasm opens, for no reason,
The chasm beneath the rose. The rose fails
To tell me anything, aphis-invaded, pink,
Just pigment. If I were to present you with a rose
Today, you'd throw it down. Last night I dreamt
Dread of a rope, hanging over the parapet.

Every day I live with a dreadful predicament:
I dare not think about it. So many words
No one has ever heard. You read one book,
Like it: we dare say nothing of publication.
So many pages I have done, so far unread.

Sorabji is a Parsee prince-composer,
Lives in Corfe Castle: published at his own expense
Scores of incredible difficulty and perplexity
No one could or would play – an oriental Scriabin.
At the end of *Opus Clavicembalisticum*
(345 pages, lasting two hours and a half)
'PUBLIC PERFORMANCE OF THIS WORK IS FORBIDDEN
BY THE COMPOSER.' John Tobin played it: fined £300.
In his will, all Sorabji's works are to be burned.

At last, someone has his permission to play something:
'This authorisation does not apply,' he writes,
'To that Execrable Institution, the BBC,
Nor to any pianist whatsoever.'
So, in his eighties, the old man cultivates
His terrible not-being-there: why do we laugh at him?

The drought-tormented plants flag in my garden.
Suppose they all turned yellow and withered?
My toe in the dusty earth, I would mourn my loss

And the breaking down of my love for the crumbly soil.
The yellowing bundles of typescript, they appal me –
A whole lifetime tied up in their staleness.
I must try not to think of them. Shall I bring you a rose?
Its yellowing delicate face, its dry sad perfume –
Won't it speak across the dusty gully between us?

The Description of a Masque & c

Pulchro pulchra datur sociali foedere amanti
*Tandem nubit amans, ecquid amabilius?**

> Eternity appeared in a long blew Taffata robe,
> With a Skye of Clowdes very arteficially shadowed.

So, too, today, midway through January,
We watched an amazing sunset, powder blue
With washed out violet bars, and seasand green
Fade into whitish gold and then again to blue,
Holding one another, lying on a soft settee,
My cheek against your cheek and my hand on your breast.

> Error first in a skin coate scaled like a Serpent:
> Rumor in a skin coate full of winged Tongues.

This week I have studied Wyatt and Ralegh,
Thumbing through the lyrics of Tho. Campion:
Horrified at the tales of their lives,
A woman, sometime lover, decapitated with an axe, seen
Through a grating in the Tower, stinking cells,
Chained up at a loss of favour, praying,
Kneeling on the cold stone; and what, I ask,
Was in Tho. Campion's mind when they sang

> Vanish, vanish hence, confusion
> Dimme not Hymens goulden light
>   With false illusion?

*'To a lovely lover is given by mutual compact a lovely woman. At
length the lover is wed – is there anything more lovable?'

– Did he know the bridal pair had administered corrosive
sublimate
To a nobleman who stood in their way,
Finishing him off with a poisoned glyster?

> For she, she, only she
> Can all knotted spels unty.

Covered with hideous sores, his tormented body
Was buried somewhere in the grounds of the Tower.
When I tell you, your jaw drops, and
That dark feminine pity comes into your eyes.

> Set is that Tree in ill houre
> That yields neither fruite nor floure.
> he confesseth that he received of alderman Helwys for
> the vse of St Thoms Mounson fourteen hundred pounds

I have nothing in my mind but the sweetness of your body,
My admiration for your quirky intelligence,
Astonishment at the winter love between us:
Yet this poetry has tormented me all week,
Records of treachery, the bitter newfangledness of women,
The cries of 'Is yt possible?', the discriminations
Against conceit and mere affection,
The dreadful dangers of that courtly sensual life:
And above all the guilt and horror
That must have been in Tho. Campion's mind.

> The Seaborne Godesse straight will come
> Quench these lights, and make all dombe.

How he must have longed for the release of sleep!

> After this Dialogue the Maskers daunce with the ladies,
> wherein spending as much time as they held fitting, they
> returned to the seats provided for them.

71

Like us, here, lying and doing nothing on the sofa
But without one anxiety in our minds,
Certainly nothing about murder, or imprisonment, or favour:
Only my troubled dreams of death, threatening
From the stone cliffs of the mountains of time
And my wish to live for ever in your arms.

> hymen doth long nights affect
> And so godnight to all, godnight to all.

FINIS